BOOK BENCHERS PUBLICATIONS
PRESENTS

OVERSOUL

Compiled By,

ASWIN S A & BERDHISHA P

AELAY PUBLICATION

A dream come true for every writers out there. We spot every possible problem for the writers, help in rectifying them and guide them towards the best outcome. We make sure to understand your needs, dreams and expectations, and nourish them with our services and stop not until we fulfill your dreams. The writers have a right and freedom to choose what they want here. They have us to guide them through the hardest path until the end. Believe in us.

Aelay Publication - by a writer for the writers.

BOOK BENCHERS

Book Benchers is the affiliate of Aelay publication. Both the publication is handled by Astro.
Aelay plays the role of publishing solo books. And Book Benchers is epically for publishing anthologies.

Book Benchers have 2 different teams.
1. Tamil

2. English/Hindi

Never mind what our main motive is to help all the budding writers, who are seeking for their dream of publishing their own book to come true.

We are there to help out everyone.
In guiding for starting up with your carrier in compiling until finishing up your full book.

COPYRIGHT

All Rights are reserved. No part of this can be reproduced, stored, copied or transmitted in any form may it be electronic, mechanical, magnetic, optical, photocopies, and or any other possible manner without the prior written approval of the writer and publication house, except for a reference in respect to the writers or the publishing entity work.

Design And Executed by

ISBN : 978-93-5533-177-9
Page : 122

ACKNOWLEDGEMENT

God Almighty deserves our gratitude for keeping us all together throughout the anthology.

We would like to express our heartfelt gratitude to the founders of Book Benchers Publication, for providing us such a wonderful opportunity to express our opinions on various aspects of the readers. We are extremely fortunate to be able to work under the auspices of this publishing house.

Furthermore, we are more thankful to the co-authors who provided detailed and constructive ideas in their write-ups.

Lastly, we would like to thank every person who directly or indirectly helped us in the completion of the book.

DISCLAIMER

This Anthology is a work of fiction. Our editors have tried their best to avoid any sort of plagiarism and the proof-readers have done their job of proof-reading best on their part to expertise the book with unplagiarized and original content. Still if any appropriation detected, the editorial team is no where responsible, the writer is solely responsible for such acts. We have well guided our co-authors to submit their original write-ups.

FOUNDER

IRUDAGA ASTRO

Irudaga Astro, From Tirunelveli, Founder of Aelay and BB (Book Benchers)

He had completed his BE.

He has written 3 Tamil poetry book's which hits the top list on social media!

His main aim is to allow the writers to publish their words as their book rather than just Posting them on Insta.

LINK AND POSTER MAKER

CATHERINE ASMI T

Catherine Asmi T, From Tirunelveli

She has completed her M.Com

Her passion is Drawing and Designing.

TEAM HEAD

She is a passionate writer from Chennai. Writing makes her pressure go away. She had played the role of co-author for more than 100+ Antho's.

She would like to thank her parents and her Loveable Brother for supporting her rather than stopping her from what she wanted to do! For being the main reason for achieving her dreams. As well as for standing beside her in all the ups and downs.

Whenever she feels like she needs to get out of her stressful timing or feels like she needs peacefulness, she starts to paint, she would never mind sitting in the same place for so many hours when it comes to her painting. She believes that anyone could hurt her, But never her books could!!

Catch her in Insta and FB

Insta: @theinnocentheart

FB: KA. PARINASRI

ASWIN S A (COMPILER)

Aswin S.A. is a budding writer. He writes in various themes exploring the true meaning of existence, connecting literature with various aspects of love and life. He writes his poems with extreme passion and all his words are filled with rhyming vividness. There is so much to learn about life from his inspiring lines. He has mastery over vocabulary and syntax, this makes his poems enjoyable. Do read the lines and enjoy for yourselves.

Insta IDs: aswin_s_a

let_me_write_something__

HER LOVE

She fell in love with His Happiness
His happiness killed the happiness in Her.

She fell in love with His Dreams,
His dreams killed the dreams in Her.

She fell in love with His innocence
His innocence killed the righteousness in Her.

She fell in love with His Possessiveness
His possessiveness made Her slave.

She fell in love with His silence,
His silence made Her to Rest in Silence.

BERDHISHA P (CO-COMPILER)

Berdhisha, born and bought up in Kaniyakumari District, Tamil Nadu. For her, it's a heaven with beautiful nature. Now she was settled down in Coimbatore. She completed her Master's Degree in Coimbatore. She is a poet who loves to share her own thoughts and imagination, which has its own uniqueness. She manifests the beauty of nature in her poems. She is a blogger; you can read her poems in http://berdhisha96.blogspot.com/ . She is a Co-author for about 100+ Anthologies, Co-author of 5 record aiming anthologies and compiling about 10 Anthologies. Her published Anthologies are "The Universal Mind", "Speculations in Solitude" and "Spicy Noodles and Cold Coffee".

Insta id : thoughts_of_mine_the_muse

LIFE WITH MY PEN

My soul pinned

By my pen

My heart speaks,

And my pen writes

When my mind thinks,

My pen describes.

When my eyes sees something,

My pen draws it as words

When my tongue speaks,

My pen crashes my thoughts

In different genre.

When my nose smells

My pen scribbles,

My hands writes

About anything

By holding my pen

OverSoul

Like my dancing legs

My pen plays with paper.

When I dream something

It will take place in my writing

When I imagine something

Some new thoughts flourished

Mixed with adventurous

I would paste it alike

In my paper

By my powerful weapon.

My pen is my king,

Thoughts hold my mind

In a wink.

I won't have a life

Without my pen.

LIST OF CO-AUTHORS:

1. Ashika S P
2. Monika M.P
3. G. Debbie Sharon
4. Abima M
5. Soubhagya S.P.
6. Ramya J
7. AayushiKhedia
8. K.M.Siva Ramya
9. Riya Richard R L
10. Anslin Dhivya .D
11. Benila S R
12. Maheltha Jaicy SD
13. Samitha S
14. Breena R. Frido
15. Jerlin Flower S
16. Gabrilla Sanchez
17. Adline Shami. M
18. Jigar Makwana
19. Anaswara A K
20. Mohammed Niyaz
21. Akash D Wise

22. J. Delinda Osheen
23. Samirkumar N. Parekh
24. L. A. Jothy Lekshmi
25. Annie P Dhas
26. Akanksha Chauhan
27. Amy Tephilla A
28. J. M. Abish Pious
29. Abi C. M
30. Bhadra . S
31. Sivaranjini M P
32. D Deena Sharmi
33. K.Sneha
34. C. Nesavathy
35. M.Sukaina
36. S. B. Sona.
37. Arthi Devi. A
38. A.S Afaya
39. Anne Benita D
40. Miss Rashmin Ghasura
41. Aathisha John Kennady
42. Gymsy Eugene
43. Gnana Shini G

44. Defency Purohit

45. Wasim Ahmad Sheergojri

46. Dharshini. M

47. Deepika Thankachy R

48. Dhanu K V

49. N C Jerushalit

50. Gayathrynair

Ashika S P

Hailing from a beautiful village Thottam, Kaniyakumari District, Tamilnadu, S. P. Ashika, holds a special interest in penning poetry. She is a polymath with multitasking talents. Her themes in poetry circulate around greenish environment, solitude and magnitude aspects of life. Her love towards the poetic world is marvelous. It's interesting to note that her thoughts as quotes are penned in b8photography.blogspot.com. Moreover, her PG dissertation is based on poetry.

SILENCE – THE LANGUAGE OF LOVE

My love waits for me in silence...

Never did he speak any words.

Utter silence it was...

But it was not silence,

It was the language of love.

He was pouring down,

His millions of trapped emotions,

All that he has failed to express in words...

The more he revealed,

The more I try to go near him.

All he expressed in a language,

That only I could understand.

Soulful isn't it? Silence –

The language of love.

Souls kiss in silence.

Monika M.P

I will start with a confession: Never did I think
that I have a thing for words and poetry until I
stepped out as a literature graduate. It was always
the poems with depth and profound intention that
caught my eyes. I started keeping a little book to
collect my favorite phrases and sentences from the
books I read. Today I am glad to be a part of this
Anthology to reveal a glimpse of what i have to
share to the world. As I look forward to embark a
writing career, I hope somewhere some reader
would find a line so close to their heart in this
poem to strike it off with a highlighter. Sending
love and warmth to my readers!

THE WHEREABOUTS

I witness stillness – the unbearable part of

existence.

Moths fluttering on monsoon nights.

The grimy electric street lamps spitting yellow

with a gentle flicker.

The pale dying evening sky light – Beckons me.

And says, 'pour!'. 'Pour your mind onto the

paper'.

What do I write when everything

I think of is a replica of dismantled human dream?

I pray to the good God to wash the morbid

vocabulary.

Tongue, brain and hands – cleansed with mirth.

Cleaning the dripping ink,

I try again/ the theory is raw again.

Let me come back to it when I know the

whereabouts of my own voice.

G. Debbie Sharon

Debbie Sharon is an aspiring writer who is a book lover. Her writings are inspired by the power of positivity in life. As she adores poetry as the subtle and thought provoking art form in the literary world she has started writing poetry. Her other interests are travel and exploring different cuisines.

NEVER GIVE UP

Never give up...

It might be your frequently heard phrase

That imbibes the spirit, which brings in praise;

How long you'll keep blaming your phase!

When it's time to build your own pace,

Until everything reflects your ace.

Once again I am here to remind you,

NEVER EVER GIVE UP as you knew,

Your strenuous efforts paint you with vibrant

hues,

And will do away with all the hardships in a blew,

As you realized that you belong to a few,

Kudos! You're on your way to make your dreams

come true!!!

Abima M

Abima is a budding writer who is very passionate in providing dreamy ideas in poetry. She finds cheer in every little thing that is deep in her heart that brings wonderful memories to her. She inspires various themes but mostly interested in shaping poems with colorful rhymes. Do enjoy the poem which may even take you to your childhood memory of that you may had with one that is very close to your heart.

MY TEDDY BEAR

A package of stuffed emotion
Where multi feelings get promotion
Language of love it shows
Fascinating thought it grows
Wonderful companion in my bitterness
And solution for my longingness
Yes! My teddy bear!
My life's gear!
It is my first childhood desire in heart
And till now, it never let me apart
Joy in every memory it gives
Heart aching anxiety it cures
It brings climax to my insecurities
And medications to my instabilities
Yes! My teddy bear!
My life's gear!

Soubhagya S.P.

Soubhagya S.P., Research Scholar of
SreeAyyappa College for Women, Chunkankadai
is a voracious reader and an upcoming writer. She
loves to write and recite poetry. Love for nature is
her eventual concern.

DEATH, THE ULTIMATE LOVER

The pain of love embraced me

Like a warm breeze

That gently strikes the petals of my heart

The dazzling sun twinkles in my eyes

With the hope of meeting that shining star

Twilight arrived showcasing the arrival of his very

existence.

The horse-driven chariot removes its curtain

Reveals the half-shadowed face of my beloved

Oh! You are that kindest thought

That stimulates my heart

Alas! My love

Shift me gently to that eternal peace

Where memory resides in peace.

Ramya J

Ramya J is professionally a teacher. Writing is her passion. The impacts of certain incidents and events make her write. It's her wish to make the readers sense those impacts. Since she is a teacher she tries to insist good values among the student community through her words. Certainly her words speak to them.

HOW GREAT OLFACTION IS!

First of all which is developed,

Ceases after you slept,

Linked highly to memory perception,

To the brain has the direct connection,

More in women exists than men,

Detects distinct odor one trillion,

Skillful to sniff fear and disgust,

In the spring and the summer being the strongest,

Weakest in the mornings, increases through the

days,

Be renewed in every thirty days,

Distinguish each except twins

Is the wondrous smelling sense.

I am in a mess

Whether to curse corona or bless

Which made me realize this,

How great olfaction is!

AayushiKhedia

Co-author AayushiKhedia is a student from Purulia, West Bengal. She can't express much and that is the reason why she started writing. She believes sometimes words speak. Through her shayaris, she tries to express her feelings. She is not a writer by profession but writing is her passion. She wrote her first shayari when she was 9 yrs old. She still remembers that day. Firstly she gives the credit to her mom. Her mother is an exceptional writer but is not famed by others. She thanks 'Your Quote' too that gave her a platform to flourish her writings. She wants to thank her father who always supported her. She wishes that he could see this and is determined to make him proud one day. She always tries to write not for fame but for the love of her readers.

IN SEARCH OF THE ONE

Up in the open sky,

Finding the one who let me fly.

Deep down in this messed up world,

Want the one who keeps everything unfurled.

Holding hands we lay down,

In our own hometown.

K.M.Siva Ramya

Siva Ramya is a student at St. Joseph's Matric Higher Secondary School in Mulagumoodu, Kanyakumari district, where she is in the 12th grade. Her hometown is in the vicinity of Azhagiamandapam. It is her desire to compose poetry, stories, quotes, and other literary works, and she is particularly interested in this. Her poems and quotes can be found on her Instagram page, ramya_km_5.

THE WORLD FROM MY WINDOW

The world is so beautiful

When I see from my window,

When I open my window,

It seems to be a amazing view

The hills and fields and falls and trees,

The charming songs of the birds can be hear,

Wow! It's amazing to see the world.

Oh,the narrow window can give an amazing view!

In each season it can give a various scene,

That makes me to go into a dreaming world,

It gives me a feeling of flying around the world,

Ah! It makes me more curious to know about the

world.

The wind blows around the trees,

It gives a amazing feeling,

It's a wonderful view -that,

I never able to forget!

Riya Richard R L

Riya Richard R. L is a young, burgeoning writer in English. She loves writing from her girlhood. Her passion and desire for writing help her to perform conscientiously. She has a unique style and distinct modus operandi in her writings. She was born in the most beautiful district Kanyakumari in the most prestigious state Tamil Nadu. She is now an undergraduate in Chemistry, doing her course in Muslim Arts College, Thiruvithancode, in her district. Besides writing, she also loves reading books, drawing, arts and crafts, and learning. She is a lover of Nature. Nature inspires her; she gets most of the ideas, thoughts, and hints from Nature.

THE PEARLS OF WISDOM

I was depressed and forsaken,

My life was full of Afflictions,

Disappointments, failures, and grief, "Why,"

I thought, I couldn't figure

In silence, my soul taught

The Pearls of wisdom

Don't lose hope in disappointments

Hope is the soul of life,

Don't lose Patience in Affliction,

Patience is the virtue of life,

Don't lose confidence in grief,

Confidence is the power of life,

Don't step backward in failures

Forward is the right direction of life

I wore the pearls of wisdom,

Now I'm a Pearl of Success in Life.

AnslinDhivya.D

A denarian named Dhivya, who is sprouting out as an ardent writer. She alleviates her grief through her inkling thoughts and quenches her thirst by the vivid verses of poetry. Her soul is well engaged with nature. The mystic verses of her cruise around everywhere in unveiling the truth.

CHILD LABOUR

Divine souls are they;

Holding the key to

Unlock the way

To plant up the barren Land with seedlings of

grin.

Heavenly charms are they;

Clasping the burden of

An aged man; sweats for a wage.

The glabrous skin,

Serving as a vast field,

To hold those massive bricks.

Deserted psyche,

Unknown to the outside world,

Days to behold;

Books to gaze upon;

A new world to seek out.

Benila S R

Mrs. Benila is a multi-talented, budding writer and erudite Scholar who loves to express her agony through writing. Aspiring to be a teacher, she is pursuing her Doctoral studies and is widely interested in Feminism.

GONE, BUT NOT FORGOTTEN

It breaks my tender heart, brother,
To accept the shattering news of your demise,
Which I received at an early morning,
That you were taken to God's paradise!

It's been a long time since seeing you,
Though separated by the force of death,
When the journey of life ends, I swear
We'll meet together with Lord.

Till then May good angels safeguard
And encircle you with their love.
May they protect and bless you
From the heavens abode.

We'll always cherish that
Innocent smile and caring heart.
Your presence on our good times
Will be remembered forever!

MahelthaJaicy SD

MahelthaJaicy SD, a Research Scholar of excellent speaking skills. Captures creative nuances and inspires lives through her writings. Very well known for her outspoken personality and being studious. a passionate writer, story teller, a lover of poetry and a great composer. Spend time with her writings and get to know about her and enrich life by making new experiences.

RECKLESS THOUGHTS

Sometimes I like to dive into the water and swim
like a fish,
From time to time I wish to fly like a bird on the
sky,
At times I like to stay in an isolated world,
Every so often, I like to possess superpowers.
Reckless thoughts tip toe into the world which
doesn't exist,
Set your soul on fire, maybe venomous, maybe
credulous,
Reckless world allures us to reckless judgments,
Those precarious firework crackers ….
Darkest or brightest, sometimes dark of the
darkest,
At times bright of the brightest,
Muddy thoughts with full of deceit,
Those hopeless emotions, how to cease them?

Samitha S

Samitha, simply a nature admirer loves to point out the pleasure which nature offers to the souls in the world every time. Her ideas are focused on how the world reacts to nature and the joy derived from nature's hand. Look through her poem and realize the relationship between nature and the human subconscious mind.

TURNOVER

The authentic aroma of nature
Rides me to the deep aura;
The fresh delicate mist
Makes over a chilling spirit,
To wake up from my snore.
Then I calmly raised my lazy eyes;
I was behind a vintage hut,
Where mountains erected their giant shoulders;
The slippery field handed a sparkle;
The spongy milk clouds,
Throws in a gleaming tickle to my eyes;
The blossoming of buds,
Charms my curious heart;
The silent rays of the Sun,
Radiates with its shyness;
The chirrup of birds,
Dazzle the breezy hills;
And the harmony of nature…
Abruptly there was some soft melody
Blowing into my ears Altering into a coarse tune,
Which made me drive out of my dream! "
Oh! It's time to wake up and
Hustle for the restless world"
That was the cockcrow reminder
From my symphonic alarm!

Breena R. Frido

Breena R. Frido is a higher secondary student, who writes short stories for children. Her characters always depict some important moral values. Her stories are always sprinkled with some fantasies. She started to identify herself as a writer from her eighth grade. Her love for writing stories is inevitable.

A TOUR TO A SPACE STATION

Long long ago, there lived a boy named Arun. He always wanted to become an Astronaut and travel to space. He was ready to do anything to achieve his dream. Seeing his strong desire for Space, his teacher always helped him with whatever he wanted. He secured first class in his higher secondary examination and got admission in a famous university to study Astrophysics. He completed his course and he did research on space science and completed doctorate in Space science. His Guide advised him to meet a famous space scientist Dr. Devendra Singh to fulfill his dream. Arun met him and expressed his strong desire to travel to space station. After a long discussion Dr.Devendra Singh agreed to help him. With his recommendation, the space committee agreed to send Arun to space. He was trained for several months on how to survive in space. At last Arun went to a space station. His research was about the "Aliens". From the first day he began to look for aliens. Somehow he found an alien. The alien too saw him and thought that he was there to destroy the aliens. It came near to him and started to attack him. He shouted and said that he would never hurt or kill it. He also told that if he tend to kill it, it can kill him. After some time the alien came near to him and started to talk to him. " I am Rex" told the alien. Arun introduced himself to the alien and they became friends. Rex asked him the reason for him to be in space. Arun told him that he was there to conduct a research on aliens. Rex smiled and said no one can be a better example than myself. He started to explain about the people, their culture, their livelihood, their food and so on. Arun completed his research successfully with the help of Rex. Finally Arun was about to leave the space station. Rex was sad to leave his best friend. He waved his hands and told him that he would miss him. Arun left the space station and returned to Earth. His research about aliens was approved by everyone and he was appreciated for his great work. Arun could not forget his dear friend Rex. He wrote a book on remembrance of his friend Rex and named it as, "A tour to a space station".

Jerlin Flower S

Jerlin Flower was born in a beautiful evergreen district of Tamil Nadu, Kanyakumari. The author now teaches English literature at the college level. As time moves on, she is learning various lessons from people around her and she shares these learnings with the world in the form of her poems. The poems reflect the thoughts of the poet beautifully. She brings out the poems deepest meaning in a lively attitude.

SILENT SCULPTOR

As a kid, her teacher ignored...

For her appearance, for being short,

Anguish in her brought in voidness.

She ignored herself-as defied by the one.

She ignored being a dancer,

She ignored being a singer,

She ignored being a speaker,

She ignored being an artist.

But evolved into a sculptor in silence.

The mastery in her was quiet,

The passion in her was quiet,

The emotion in her was quiet.

But, the TEACHER - her inborn nature,

Made every friend honour her ignorance!

Made every student love her ignorance!

Made her herself in ignorance!!

Gabrilla Sanchez

Gabrilla Sanchez is a free verse writer who expresses the valley of emotions in a different perspective. Her poems explicate the truth about life and you can check out her Instagram page @dreamgirlgaby. Life is a mixed emotions which lets you to face bitter truths and also the beautiful sides of happiness by surprising you in little moments. Let's explore it and mature together.

THE NEVER-ENDING FIGHT

Life, the never-ending fight,
Each stage surpassed with highest goals,
To glorify the standards of living,
The never-ending fight,
Causes the conscience to disappear,
To sustain the high-profile positions,
The never-ending fight,
Values the money over relationships,
Showing off the pride over humanity,
The never-ending fight,
Originates the comparison,
Resulting the loss of one's self-uniqueness,
The never-ending fight,
Is the life cannot be parted until death,
Humans being compared on a scale,
The top is treated with respect and gets the best,
The bottom is treated with shame and gets the
worst,
The never-ending fight,
Indicates life as an endless race,
With a load of competitors and competitions,
The untold truth;
Run until you win,
As life is a never-ending fight.

AdlineShami. M

AdlineShami is a lover of birds. She is also an opacarophile. Her poem displays her tenderness nature and affection towards the birds. To set her mind free from expectations and to avoid broken trust in humans, she conveys a message of love which can never be broken when you have a pet.

ODE ON MY MAJESTY

Here, she saunters in her charm,

Doesn't cause any harm,

Flaunting in grey and yellow,

Singing a melody mellow.

Dainty blush of orange cheek,

Her wondrous eyes, they never fail to speak,

Oh! She wears a majestic crown,

Not of gold; nor precious stone.

She exalts on her throne,

Magnificent excellence she own,

Oh dear Lord! My Queen is maimed,

Oh! It is such a shame!

Fret not my majesty, you'll be fine,

For healing, they're divine!

Paten is on what you dine,

You never scorn plates of mine.

Should you be in a cage confined?

No, no more a captive, free and refined,

Oh! Ye good people! I shall tell,

She is Buji; my majestic Cockatiel!

Jigar Makwana

Jigar Makwana is a PhD Research scholar, Lecturer, Blogger and Poet. He hails from Ahmadabad, Gujarat, India. He is featured in "World's First Book on Haiku Poetry". He is the editor and compiler of "The Rising Channel's Anthology". His writing is based on real events and sometimes he expresses supernatural elements in his writing. Blog: www.jigarmakwana.wordpress.com

MEMORIES OF YOU

I am in memories of you, for that lovely moment.

There is lots of love in a way,

In time by time;

Moment of moment,

I lost you in present.

We love each other,

But what shall we do.

The road is endless,

We feel the loneliness.

Because our memories,

In past that we passed way;

Nothing that really comes away.

I don't know you meet,

But in memories we meet.

Anaswara A K

The Author of this poem is Miss. AnaswaraA K. She is a school student, very much interested in writing poems. She is brilliant in her curricular as well as Co-curricular activities.

THIS SHALL TOO PASS

Remembering the past…
The days we gathered together
In schools, Offices and other occasions
Everywhere filled with joy and happiness

Special memories with Family and Friends
That never fades though the time passes
Never imagined the situation
Which the world is passing through

No festivals no celebrations
Only safety and precautions
Inside home with online communications
Saluting the warriors fighting for us

Let's believe, this shall too pass
Let's unite together to fight against this
Our protector will protect us
And shower us with Love and care.

Mohammed Niyaz

Mohammed Niyaz hails from Mumbai - The City of Dreams. He often loves to write poetries and short music video stories for his own youtube channel. Apart from this Mohammed is currently working on his upcoming anthologies, as well writing poetries since 2013. You can find him on facebook/mohammedniyaz as well on instagram @niyazsks.

THE PANDEMIC WAVES

We all were unaware of the upcoming storm.

When it started with the speed of tuning form.

The crises started with cases being toping the numbers.

That weren't lacking from the crossed of climbers.

And the whole world was in a state of lockdown.

Areas which were locked from the cities and town.

Deaths was now having an agreement with tolls.

Which never misleaded in the rolls.

We all experienced the toughest times till date.

With no clues of what will be our fate.

Choosing wisely the decisions of saves.

From first, second and until "the pandemic waves".

Akash D Wise

Akash D Wise is a player, writer, photographer and a person who likes to express all his lovable feelings in the form of poems and short stories. He is very interested in wrestling and a healthy diet. I don't know more about him but he is a admirable poet with great sense of feelings in his poems.

FOR MY TREASURE

A notably little girl with a sweet face

Entered my heart at the first glance,

My eyes stopped blinking and started to gaze,

Even my hands and legs started to dance,

My mind was lost on her eyes of blaze.

She started to stare at my steady stance,

I lost my solidity by her single blink,

She made my anger and sadness shrink.

One day everything will turn fine,

When I hold your hand and say "you are mine".

J. Delinda Osheen

J. Delinda Osheen is a Ph.D. Research Scholar, also working as an Assistant Professor in English. She is interested in writing poems and quotes. She writes under the pen name Delinda Aldrin.

DEAR ME

It's okay when things fall apart;

It's okay if nothing was in its place;

It's okay to hangout with setbacks;

It's okay to feel like giving up;

It's okay to go through afflictions and hardships.

But, Remember Who you are?

You are Unique! You are Capable!

You are out of the Ordinary!

You are Beautiful inside out! You are Awesome!

Be Kind, Have Courage;

Tuck your vibe tight, Button your attitude right;

Pin your hope high, Set your sky to fly;

Ignore the haters because YOU maters.

Samirkumar N. Parekh

He is working as an Assistant Professor at College
in Navsari, Gujarat.

BETWEEN US..!

How can I be at Peace...?

When you are not at ease...!

Whether you tell or not,

I know there are some knots..!

But, between us,

Words are mere customary,

Feelings are our custody..!

Though you are not near,

I feel your worries here...!

Prayers are always with you,

This is the best I can do...!

L. A. JothyLekshmi

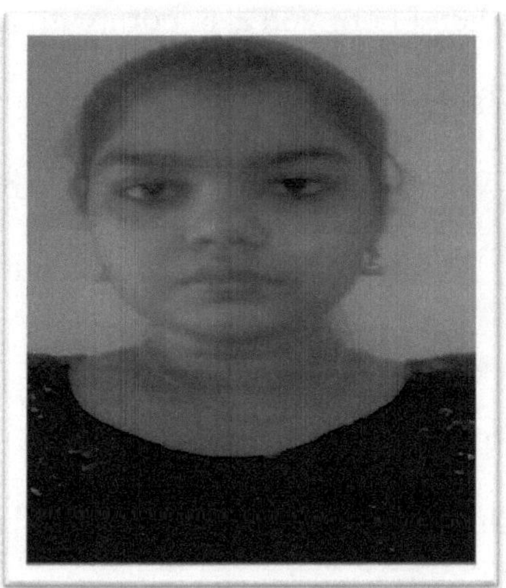

L.A.JothyLekshmi is a budding writer. Her poems are very interesting. She has written many poems in Tamil. She is a good artist and a creative writer too.

MY SHADOW FRIEND

When I born you also born with me

When I laugh you too laugh with me

When I cried you cried with me

I think you're the best gift that

God had given me

Sorry for searching for a true friend

Without knowing you're my best friend

And I know, our journey of friendship never end

Annie P Dhas

Annie . P. Dhas is a school student interested in expressing her feelings through poems. She has special interest in singing and writing poems. Her theme in poem is about her sweet sister and the love towards her.

SWEET SISTER

One fine day,

I found Her-stranger

Have never been travelled before

But blessings on the air

Started a new joy of travel,

A special trust of love

Everyone has a wonderful sister,

But, Why such a treasure for me?

So I begin to thank the maker

Hard to know, does she likes me

But she'll be there in all my tomorrows.

Akanksha Chauhan

Akanksha Chauhan is a reader writer and a student of literature. She writes on love and relationship. Especially her work is a mirror of untold expression of human personna. Through her poetry she recalls the memory. She uses some natural elements to connect deeply.

POETRY OF HER OWN WORLD

Yeah! She is poetry,
Thousand words in her heart,
She is full of scars!
Her body is the mirror of her sorrow.
Judgment of her character; has already made by
Society. People feel ashamed,
When she speaks!
For her teary eyes,
She forgot; She has no rights.
Oh love! Please, Be in distance;
She is made just for breath,
Her rosey lips now turned dry.
She asks, the sky;
Can I fly?
Yeah! She is a poetry,
But, none can read!
Her scars has permanent place,
Her soul tells to never escape.
Now, she is breathing with joy;
She knows, she is not a toy!
Why should she prove Her;
If, none is valued her presence.
Yeah! she is a poetry;
A poetry of her own world!

Amy Tephilla A

Amy Tephilla is a person who loves to express her
heart out. She believes that message can be
conveyed better through writing than speaking.
She expresses her thoughts and motivates herself
through her writings.

THE WILD

I was in the lonely dark place
Cold and shivering
Far away
Deserted in an abandoned Island
Where am I?
Oh dear me
I am lost
What should I do?
Trampling in the dark paths
Getting bruised in my body
Darkness gives a pain in my body
Heaviness on me pushes me down
What should I do?
I am gonna give up
I keep thinking that I can't do it
Someone help me, please
I am dependent
That's it I give up..
Wait what?
Give up?
Where in the world?
Is that it?
Cry out girl
The wild inside me is coming out
Like the roar of the tiger
The fiery look in my eyes
Sparks the dark with light

The wounds on me give the fierce
Setting my feet firm on the ground
Making my rough path to my destiny
The wild in me is going wild
I am out for battle the dark
I am stronger to smash the beast out there
Here I am strong and wild
Making my way to my destiny.

J. M. Abish Pious

J. M. Abish Pious was born in the natural beauty district Kanyakumari, Tamil Nadu. He completes Bachelor of Divinity and working as a pastor in a Lutheran Church. He loves to write poem and devotional lyrics. He writes actively Self-Assertive Verses, Poems and Articles in the social media and blog. Especially his writings are mostly based on Love, Justice, Peace and Equality in the society. To follow his writings through facebook.com/abish.pious& abishpious.blogspot.com.

SINGLE SANDALS!

Hey, Single sandal !

What do you think about me?

I Can't walk,

I sit in the chair.

I Can't run,

I take rest in the chair.

I Can't jump-

I joined new life.

In life, I spun like a wheel.

When I Stuck in the vehicle's wheel,

Later, I browse in a wheelchair,

Something I lost to wear sandals,

Useless Sandals for the Foot.

Right or Left,

Single foot sandals!

Abi C.M

Abi.C.M is a budding writer. She writes in various theme, connecting literature of nature, life and other many things. She writes her poems with extreme passion and all her words are filled with rhyming vividness .do read the lines and enjoy for yourselves

THE EARTH WE LIVE IN

The life on the Earth is beautiful;

I think it is wonderful!

No one knows about the Earth's mystery;

When we find out, it makes the history!

The fruit of life is delicious;

The gift given by Earth is precious!

To continue this creatures, we need heir;

So, I find the life on Earth is fair!

The three-fourth of Earth is filled with water;

How we use our mother Earth is matter!

The nature donars are tree;

As they gave oxygen free!

Do not allow the Earth to be a waste;

Then your life will be lost!

The Earth is the place where I live in;

So love the Earth we live in!

Bhadra . S

She is a Nature lover. She likes to travel around the whole world. She likes to read many short stories. She likes painting and art works. She loves her family more than everything in the world .She likes to make many friends.

I HAVE A BEAUTIFUL ANGEL WITH ME AND I CALL HER MOM

I have a beautiful angel with me and I call her mom. A mom is the precious gift for all the living creatures of this world .She is the queen of all creatures. I always felt that she is the life of house because if she is not there for a few minutes it seems that the house is dead. She is the only person in the world whom I never wish to miss at anytime. I can't imagine a single day without her. She is like a shadow who always stays with me in all situations. She brings me to this world with a lot of pain and I that it must be her last cry for me .She is always a good friend for me in my life . She is the only person in the world who I can tell all my secrets without fear. She is my everything. Mother is a person who can take the place of all other but nobody can replace her. Finally she is the pillow of our house. To the whole world, she is the mother but for our family she is the world.

Sivaranjini M P

Sivaranjini M P was born in the district of Kanyakumari, Tamil Nadu. She is a person who is interested in exploring the world of art and literature. She has completed her Master of Philosophy degree in English Literature. In her spare hours, she utilizes her time by writing verses and quotes, and also very much interested in pencil sketching.She is also interested in reading books and writing reviews. During her Post-graduation, she had included herself in the Rotary club that tied with her institutions. She had also have participated in intercollegiate quiz competition and had won second prize. During her Mphil she had published articles as a part of her research. To know more about her, follow her (latharanjini_24)

STRUGGLES AND HOPE

Grasping hold of the weakest twigs
To climb up from a deepest pit
Along with the thorns in the branches
That creates unhealing wounds and scratches

With no other hand to hold me up
I'm struggling the unending struggles
All the pain I carry in my heart
Pushing me down into a deepest vault

Hanging in between life and dead-end
My mind thinks of the hope that drained
Beyond the misty mountains of hardships and pain
Moving far away from me leaving just a stain

Restoring all the strength I gain
When the wind of hope blows again
I started climbing from the grave of vain
To the highest peak of a strong mountain.

D Deena Sharmi

She is a budding writer. She opens her mind
through her pen. Her lines reflect the real world.
Explore her writings to explore the world.

WILL I FIND MYSELF

I'm lost deep in thoughts;

Recalling my memories.

When people were together,

The Earth with perfect atmosphere,

The trees were our best friends,

No worries; no jealousy; no threats.

The pure hearts with only happiness,

Memories mesmerize me,

But, now reality hits People are selfish,

United only with gadgets,

Fake smile; fake love & fake relationships.

A life behind the golden bars,

Nothing is real, I want to be real,

But, will I find myself?

K.Sneha

K.Sneha was born in 2004 in Tamil Nadu, South India . Growing up she was fascinated with shuttle,and this interest led to some early exposure to reading and writing. Sneha considers her faith and family to be most important to her. She starts to write more about family and friends.If she isn't spending time with her friends and family you can almost always find her around reading calm and sweet part of books. FRIENDSHIP is Sneha's first poetry

FRIENDSHIP

My friend beautify my life,

Like a shining star in the sky.

Who knows me well,

Cheers me up.

When I am in trouble,

You boost my life with smile.

Sometimes we fought together but;

If we sit for a while,

We will make each other smile.

You're my dearest friend,

And our friendship will never end.

C. Nesavathy

C. Nesavathy, Assistant Professor of English teaches at Holy Cross College, Nagercoil. She is a bibliophile and green panther. She designed a life she loved. She lost herself in literature. She believes she makes a different kind of world with her notion of literature. She is unstoppable. Her secret of success is that she did it all with passion. She is a creator, yes, she gives life to the literary characters through teaching. Wherever she goes she sows creative thinking.

LOVE

Sprouts in the hearts of brave

Yet many may remain naive

From ancient to modern

Fencing and wrestling to prove

Bards played with spellbound breve

The secret song of Adam and Eve

Transcends worldly elements of five

Grows and lives even in cave

To them, sardius, topaz, and sapphire it gave

Mesmerising moments and memories

Travels blood, bone and nerve

Offers the power and courage to move

But never the heart to leave

More and more they give

And stay together beyond the grave.

M.Sukaina

M.SUKAINA is a budding writer and co author of many anthologies. She is pursuing her UG in Muslim Arts College, Thiruvithancode. She lives in a greenery world called Colachel. Her poem based on emotions and feelings. Most of her poem is sad truth.Interested to know more about her follow on her Insta handle @sukaina kuraish.

HOMELESS LONELINESS

I heard the pleasing air

I learn the tuning voice of birds

They remind me that "am always here for you"

When I spot the sky,

It makes me to shy I bowed my head with smile

That overly remind me "am with you"

Again I heard, listen and

I realize the words "Am with you ,am always here
for you"

I smile inside because now the glorious words

I heard By my homeless Loneliness.

S. B. Sona

S. B Sona is pursuing Higher Secondary education. She has been developing the habit of writing and reciting poems right from her Childhood. Moreover, she is a social reformer and her lines convey some concern for the society.

COVID--19

Corona Virus, the worst disease,
Hide in your homes, if you please.
A disease killing lives,
And spreading negative vibes,
Symptoms like fever making us weak,
Doctor's help, we need to seek.
Started in China, now, the world if sick,
Let us unite and find a cure, quick.
We can't go to malls,
Nor can we go to waterfalls,
Because this virus is a - scaring,
Sending our spines into a shivering.
If you have to go out, think twice,
Wear your mask, be wise.
After coming home, sanitize,
And wash your hands thrice.
COVID--19 is the name,
It is playing a hide-and-seek game,
Don't go to crowd places,
Don't be one of those thousand cases,
Sneeze and cough into a tissue,
Let's take some steps to tackle this issue.
Visit a doctor if you need care,
Now, just make others, all aware.

A. Arthi Devi

Arthi Devi. A. is a literary scholar with ardent zeal for writing. An introvert who finds solace in expressing her thoughts through writing. She gives her readers a dreamy treat with her short stories by exploring the themes of self discovery, spirituality, childhood and fantasy. Her stories have a unique touch that shifts the readers to a highly imaginative world. Do read her stories to have a ride into a fantasy world.

DREAMS ARE MORE FASCINATING THAN REALITY

Theme: Friendship

And in the beginning of Spring, in a breezy morning she was sleeping peacefully by cuddling her teddy amidst the chirping of swallows. And all of a sudden, she was disturbed by her friends' cheerful yelling, "Happy Holi Aura!!" She woke up and found everyone with strange faces. At first, she couldn't recognize their faces for a second because they were smeared in different vibrant colors. She was not able to control her laughter and abruptly Ellu splashed some coloured water on her face. Following her Swetha, Alice and Arjun started to sprinkle all the blazing colours on her. The girl along with her friends and all other children from the apartment, with full zeal and happiness on their flawless innocent faces went to the garden. They started their day by throwing colours playfully on each other and got fully drenched in colours, pretty much resembling zombies. The whole day was spent colorfully and every nook and corner of the apartment was filled with happy laughter of children. The places wherever they stepped in was filled with colour. On the other side, the elders shared sweets and expressed their love, compassion and gratitude. The 'Fab 5 friends', (that's how they labeled themselves) jumped into the pool and the scared one 'Alice' was pushed by others into the pool who was scared of depth but the most interesting thing was none of them know how to swim. Some alluring songs were blasted to add some fun and they danced with graceful moves. Hours went by and the scorching sun came up with his bright rays. They dined together after long days and enjoyed their lip smacking delicious lunch along with some chit-chats. They also exchanged few valuable gifts as well. In the evening, they watched a horror movie and played pranks by scaring one another. And when the four tried to scare Aura, by wearing a spooky Halloween mask, she screamed and woke up... (that means she was dreaming and her dream gets shattered). And when she realized that all her happy moments were just her dream, she wished "if it happens one day how it would be??" Then with a regretful smile on her face, she started her routine work.

A.S Afaya

Afaya is a person who is interested in creating new contents which is eye catching for the readers. Her passion is to personify the nature with humans and show the interdependency of humans to nature. She has moulded herself in creative content writing and she also expresses her views through her writings. The main idea which holds in her writing is human feelings. She makes sure not to bring boredom onto the readers' .And she works hard to expressing her views apt and to the point. She is working on her skills to perceive the writing as her career.

THE RAIN DROPS

Pitter patter raindrops, pouring down unexpected.

Pitter patter raindrops, banging at the roof tops.

Pitter patter raindrops, welcomed with a warm
smile.

Pitter patter raindrops, splashing on the foot paths.

Pitter patter raindrops, flooding up the field
grounds.

Pitter patter raindrops, flowing through the street
loops.

Pitter patter raindrops, cleaning up the whole
world.

Pitter patter raindrops, we love you for now and
then.

Anne Benita D

Anne Benita is a budding author who loves to write poems. Her first book "The Hidden Reality of Life" carries the themes of reality. She wishes to write on such themes.

TRUTH OF LIFE

Hearing the bells of mourning,

Heart halt for a while from chiming;

White lilies were over me,

Startled by the sight to see;

I looked handsome in that box,

But heard the dreadful howl of fox.

Flew high with the angels of dark,

Lost myself from the man of hark;

Darkness wrapped, howl of hell heard,

Merriness of earth turned;

I woke up from my dreadful dream

With the fear of truth of life from dreamy stream.

Miss. Rashmin Ghasura

Herself RashminGhasura, an Assistant Professor.
Besides, she would like to introduce herself as a
researcher as well as a writer. She is a great lover of
nature. She has received many prizes in writing poems
and essays at school and College level. She has
completed M.Phil by doing research in feminism.
Now, she is exploring herself in the field of literature
through creative writing. Her interest of areas are
feminism, diaspora, mysticism and day to day life
issues. Further, she has a telegram channel to help
students. She likes to mingle both facts and fancies in
her writings. She is passionately writing research
article, poems and short stories. She likes to teach
LSRW to language learners. Reading, writing,
gardening and painting are her hobbies.

DREAMS

I have planted dreams
Come pick the petals.
It is scattered under the eyelids
Come weave petals.
One night's sleep
The first watch of the second watch
The third one after the fourth one
Hundreds of millions filled the shamans
It is used to treat the eyelids
The petals will knock.
I have captured the dreams
Come meet the petals.
The gold is sold in silver
The knitting is intertwined with the strings of the
dill
The tension of memories is woven.
Hope is painted with the colours of despair.
It is easy to love.
Wings feathers.
I have decorated my dreams
The petals come lightly.
I have planted dreams
Come pick the petals.

Aathisha John Kennady

Aathisha John Kennady is a poet who brings out the common feeling in an elite manner. The most inspirational aspect is that the readers get themselves emotionally attached to the poem which is an achievement for the writer. We all know that common feeling can never be said, but Aathisha here makes a brilliant stunt by expressing the common feelings through her poem.

MY LITTLE CANINE

I chuckled at the little man,
Wriggling around my hand,
Licking my face to let him go,
Numbing my thumb to release him,
What a canine he was!

All I feel now is numb,
Apathetic, and bare.
My eyes keep on projecting,
The last moment, I spent
With my little canine.

In his stretcher, My little one,
Breathed his last, gazing at me.
As I saw his eyes losing his soul,
I stepped closer stroking his head,
And tried to ease his pain.

I could hear the machines,
Going crazy all over the room
Bowing my head,
All I thought was,
"What do I do without him!"

Gymsy Eugene

She is Gymsy, hailing from Nagercoil. Currently, she is pursuing Master of Philosophy in English Literature. She gives life to thoughts through words.

THE SMILE

Not all the smiles,

Means the same;

Not all the smiles,

Express the joy;

Not all the smiles,

Are the sign of happiness;

Not all the smiles,

Symbolise a happy person;

Not all the smiles,

Are from the heart.

Not all the smiles.....

Few smiles,

To pretend Happy;

Few smiles,

To hold back tears;

Few smiles,

To stop explaining;

Few smiles,

To hide the pain.

Keep smiling.

Gnana Shini G

Architect by Profession! Writer by Passion!!
Passionate, introverted human being from
Southern tip of India. Connect to know me more
@ pan_da_girl

OUR TINY TALES

Some bonds are purely magical!

You never know how and when did that happen,

But it happened for good!

Just so much love!

She inked;

He captured;

They made stories forever!!!

Some stories are hidden deep inside the chambers

of the heart!

Nor said nor forgotten!!

You are my favorite story,

I love re reading our chapters;

Anytime, anyday!

Always and Forever!!

Defency Purohit

She is Defency Purohit, a Post Graduate in English Literature from The Maharaja Maharaja Sayajirao University of Baroda. She has been served as an Assistant Professor of English at Parul University for four years. Writing for me has been an expression of the inner self as well as of the outer world. I have written poems, short stories that have been published in magazines of the Parul University. I also have few research papers published in peer reviewed journals.

IN TO THE ABYSS

A naive little boy jumped to and fro;

On the coolest blades,

Swam across the lake nearby,

And appeared fresh as 'dew'.

Onto the swing, he swirled,

Slided on the mountain bridges,

Carrying the Jamuns, honey, flowers

And sweet fragrance of the earth,

Nothing more than contentment he earned.

The world opened to him from a tiny little box

For days and years then;

The mountains, the meadows and the lake waited,

Seeking the outmost presence of the boy

Who watched life now from a device;

A phone, a phone it is!

Consumed him already.

Wasim Ahmad Sheergojri

Wasim Ahmad Sheergojri did his B Ed. and M A from University of kashmir. At, present, he is doing Ph. D from MANUU, Hyderabad. He has presented his research papers in various National and International conferences. He has publication in UGC Care list.

DREAM

I saw a dream,

I saw a dream

Playing children in a mean,

A leader with paws joined be

With superior trainers in an aim

Dictating the rules on we.

Alter our play in a chor

Intially we did it so in a jolly low

By getting a confection when we bore

Saying their bylaws and more

No wise we receive in our bow.

Questioned this to the leader why it so

Answered he sweetly it was not so.

The act acts in their way

Look Allah is only our pray

What can we may, what can we say.

Dharshini. M

She is Dharshini from kovilpatti. She is pursing masters in English. She has huge interest in writing. She loves to share her thought and emotion through her writing.She has done many anthologies as co author. She has published a book named 'Vox of mine '.

GIFTS

Gifts are the valuable thing

It's a express of love

It's may be little or huge

It's carries an endless love

In the form of the present

The duration of selecting a gift

Is fully occupy of their thoughts

Evolves the mind and their wish list

Runs in the slower pace

To catch up a perfect gift

More than receiving,

Giving present make me happier

Deepika Thankachy R

Deepika a young poet who grown by knowing pain all around and that pain made her to take a pen to write. From Pain to Fantasies she weigh down all her heaviness and happiness onto the paper and make it as beautiful as she can. Got a pen to write.

CAN SOMEONE?

A deep bottomless chasm through my heart...

By thinking again;

Maybe someone can fix,

The broken pieces,

By thinking again;

Maybe one day someone,

Take the pain away,

Maybe one day...

At the end of the day by realizing that,

The broken pieces can't be fixed...

Byrealizing that,

The pain can't be taken away... '

Cause day by day,

It may break me again...!

Dhanu K V

Dhanu K V was born in Kanyakumari, Tamil Nadu. She has completed her degree in Master of Philosophy in English Literature. She is a Blogger, Bookstagrammer and currently working as a Research Analyst in her native. In her leisure hours, she spends her quality time by reading, writing poetry, writing book reviews and creating content. She loves music, Indian classical dance, especially bharathanatyam and every art form with aesthetic appeal. expresses her emotions through the form of words.

To know more about her, follow her on
https://www.dhanutravel.wordpress.com
https://www.instagram.com/dhanu_scribblings
https://www.instagram.com/dhanu_reads

IMPERFECT HARMONY

It feels like, as if I haven't slept for years.
I am so weary with existence;
Tired of everything that I am doing these days.
It just feels like to have a long vacation:
Because it's huffing here to breathe out,
With some peace or any presence!
I don't want to engulf myself
Into heap of my miseries
And sobering all the day.

I sat there and there and there...
Time is ticking as each moment passes!
Wind caress my mane with its soft touch
And brought me back to reality.
I then sneak my gaze out through my window
The evening breeze once again brushes my
cheeks.
And the smile rouses on my lips,
With the beautiful sight of setting sun;
With the rays of hope.
After all life is being balanced
In midst of imperfect harmony!

N C Jerushalit

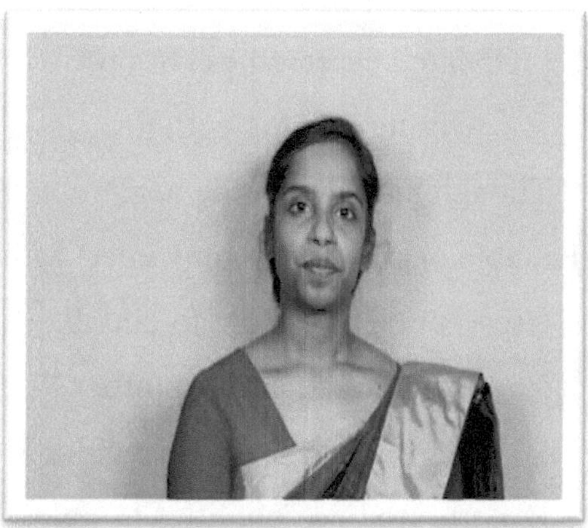

A passionate soul comprehending life's battles with a positive eloquence. Pens down lines to energize and elevate people, directing them to achieve and cling to God.

LET'S INAUGURATE

Opening ceremonies cut open

Obscure works with joy

Though pain marks the beginning

Humble beginning accompanied with

Great turns, transform to tantalize

Young minds to explore

Youthful spirits to entertain

Experienced personalities to train

The aching and aspiring souls

To quench their thirst for creativity

To qualify their minds for confidentiality-And

To explore the inherent talents for courtesy

We are all creators in our own way

Planning and proceeding to blossom

As a bud ready to bloom

To spread its fragrance

Let our minds get ignited to initiate

Let our thoughts start its count

To cover up the exploited world

To transform it with storming ideas

This might pain making a heart frozen and frenzy

Let the fire burn To make, mold and motivate

Mourning minds with new victories

Mastering minds with new discoveries

Hilarious in thought and action

Hitting the goal to achieve

Not the least Not the better

But the best,

Best to break the hurdles

Let it prove to be an enduring inauguration

To each and everyone

Who loves to conquer complements

And inherit the heights of fame

Where sky will not be their limit.

Gayathrynair

S.L.Gayathry was born in paradise of nature, Kanyakumari, Tamil Nadu. She is an artistic person and endorses herself into the world of art. She has completed her Master's degree in English Literature. In her leisure hours, she kills her time by writing stories and poetry, art making and more than to her elated excitement, she plays Ghatam and Mridangam. During her Post-graduation, she held in the position of President of Rotaract club that tied with her institutions and had organized many social services. To know more about her, follow her (gayathry.nair)

FRAGRANCE OF LOVE

Snow balls falls on Earth as honor

Green sprouts give Breath as popper

Amid beauty of Spring are known

Grains on land were empty source

Violet viper suddenly gets off

Virtuous beauty landed so far

Awning shatters for a while

Amble beauty, my dear love

Fairy breeze almost done

Melt me like anvigourlous nun

Privet sharps often profane

Coffin opens lanes and streets

Show me something dark and dusk

Shivering hands of love and lust

Certain figer outs rationally shown

Cunning eyes with full of glows

Finding way to lively go on

Lovely! Lovely! Hatered so far!

OverSoul

OverSoul